Divali

Nancy Dickmann

www.raintreepublishers.co.uk
Visit our website to find out
more information about
Raintree books.

To order:
☎ Phone 0845 6044371
📄 Fax +44 (0) 1865 312263
📧 Email myorders@raintreepublishers.co.uk

Customers from outside the UK please telephone +44 1865 312262

Raintree is an imprint of Capstone Global Library Limited, a company incorporated in England and Wales having its registered office at 7 Pilgrim Street, London, EC4V 6LB – Registered company number: 6695582

Text © Capstone Global Library Limited 2011
First published in hardback in 2011
The moral rights of the proprietor have been asserted.

Edited by Sian Smith, Nancy Dickmann, and Rebecca Rissman
Designed by Steve Mead
Picture research by Elizabeth Alexander
Production by Victoria Fitzgerald
Originated by Capstone Global Library Ltd
Printed and bound in China by South China Printing Company Ltd

ISBN 978 0 431 00712 0
14 13 12 11 10
10 9 8 7 6 5 4 3 2 1

British Library Cataloguing in Publication Data
Dickmann, Nancy.
 Divali. -- (Holidays and festivals)
 1. Divali--Pictorial works--Juvenile literature.
 I. Title II. Series
 394.2'6545-dc22

Acknowledgements
We would like to thank the following for permission to reproduce photographs: Alamy pp. **7** (© discpicture), **8** (© Tim Gainey), **9** (© Mary Evans Picture Library), **16** (© Visage), **19**, **23 bottom** (© Peter Brown), **20**, **23 top** (© Art Directors & TRIP), **21** (© Louise Batalla Duran); Corbis pp. **10** (© Historical Picture Archive), **17** (© Mark Bryan Makela); Getty Images pp. **6**, **23 bottom** (Narinder Nanu/AFP), **14** (Asif Hassan/AFP); Photolibrary pp. **4** (India Picture), **5**, **23 top** (Mohammed Ansar/Imagestate), **11**, **12**, **15** (Photos India), **13** (Alex Mares-Manton/Asia Images); Shutterstock pp. **18** (© jamalludin), **22 top left** (© Ronald Chung), **22 top right** (© Nir Levy), **22 bottom left** (© Stephane Breton), **22 bottom right** (© Mahantesh C Morabad).

Front cover photograph of traditional pooja thali reproduced with permission of Photolibrary (Hemant Mehta/India Picture RF). Back cover photograph reproduced with permission of Photolibrary (Photos India).

We would like to thank Diana Bentley, Dee Reid, Nancy Harris, and Richard Aubrey for their invaluable help in the preparation of this book.

Every effort has been made to contact copyright holders of material reproduced in this book. Any omissions will be rectified in subsequent printings if notice is given to the publishers.

Contents

What is a festival?

A festival is a time when people come together to celebrate.

Hindu people celebrate Divali in the autumn.

Sikh people also celebrate Divali.

diva lamp

Divali is called the Festival of Lights. Special lamps are lit.

The story of Divali

Rama

Sita

Long ago, there was a prince called Rama. He had a wife called Sita.

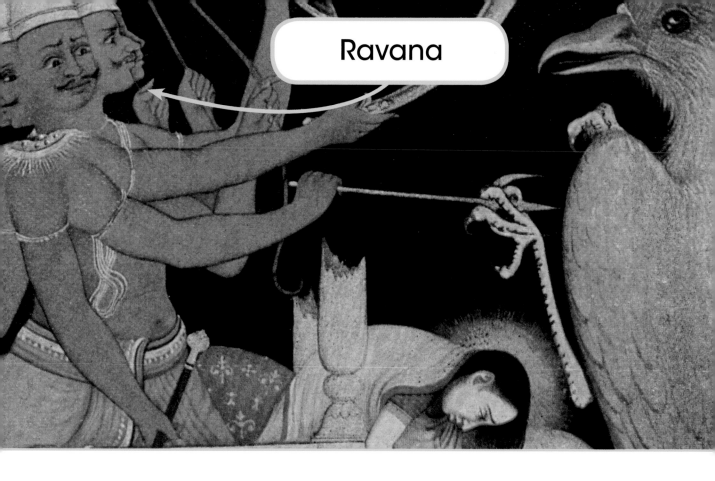

Ravana

Sita was taken away by a wicked king.
He was called Ravana.

9

Rama beat Ravana in a battle.
Sita was then able to come home.

People lit lamps to show Rama and Sita the way home.

Celebrating Divali today

At Divali, some people think of the story of Rama and Sita.

Some people think of other stories about good beating evil.

diva lamp

People light lamps in their homes.

People draw pictures on their doorsteps.

People give cards and presents.

People dance and play music.

People watch fireworks.

mandir

People go to the mandir.

People welcome Lakshmi.

They hope she will bring good luck for the next year.

Things to look for

diva lamp

fireworks

Lakshmi

pictures

Have you seen these things? They make people think of Divali.

Picture glossary

 **Hindu people** people who follow the teachings of the religion Hinduism

 **Lakshmi** Hindu goddess of wealth and good fortune

 **mandir** building where Hindus worship together

 **Sikh people** people who believe in the teachings of the gurus. The gurus were important holy men in India.

Index

Notes for parents and teachers

Before reading

Ask the children if they know what holidays and festivals are. Can they name any festivals they celebrate with their families? Discuss the difference between ordinary holidays and religious festivals. Explain that Divali is a festival celebrated by Hindu people, who follow the religion of Hinduism and by Sikh people, who follow the religion of Sikhism. Divali is sometimes spelt with a 'w' (see page 14) and sometimes spelt with a 'v' but both words refer to the same festival. Divali is called the Festival of Lights.

After reading

• Read *Rama and the Demon King* by Jessica Souhami to the children. Explain that for many people Divali is about the triumph of good over evil. Ask the children to think about the characters in the story. Which of them fit with the ideas of goodness or evil?

• Talk about diva lamps and things that light can stand for such as goodness, hope, and wisdom. Tell the children about other religions that use light as a symbol, such as the Jewish festival of Hanukkah. Show the children photos of divas and help them to design their own.

• Talk about Divali as a time of optimism or hope and new beginnings. Discuss how this fits with traditional Divali activities such as cleaning houses, sowing crops, or wearing new clothes. Ask the children to think of ways that they could make a 'new beginning'. You could suggest ideas such as sorting out differences with schoolmates, starting a new project, or cleaning their room.